Ellie Changes Colour

by Dawn Riley

This book is dedicated to

Leighton
and her best friend, Ellie

Ickerly

Wickerly

Wooooo

Ellie's the colour...

BLUE

Wickity

Wockity

Weeen

Ellie's the colour...

GREEN

Happily

Dapperly

Edddd

Ellie's the colour...

RED

Yockity

Dockity

Dellow

Ellie's the colour...

YELLOW

slipperty

sloperty

slurple

Ellie's the colour...

PURPLE

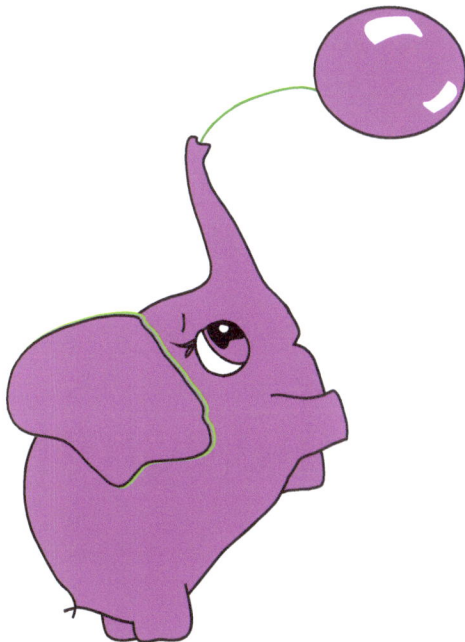

Tinkerly

Winkerly

Light

Ellie's the colour...

WHITE

Tipperty

Topity

Tink

Ellie's the colour...

PINK

Pickerty
Pockerty
Porrange

Ellie's the colour...

ORANGE

Hoppity

Doppity

Dak

Ellie's the colour...

BLACK

Colours

Colours

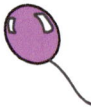

Colours

Ellie is all the colours...

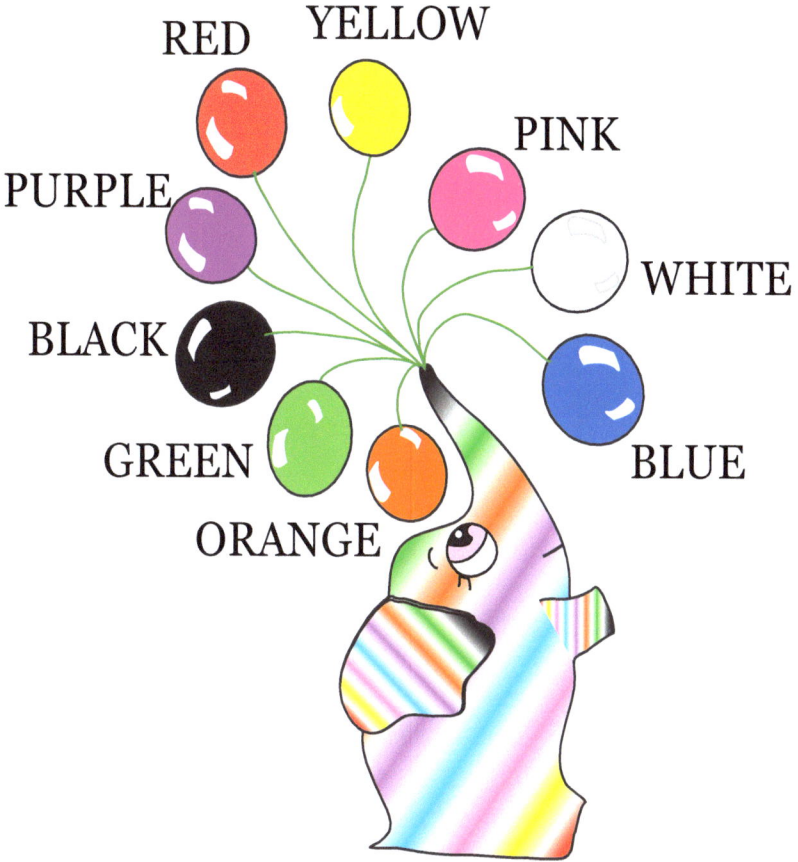

RED

YELLOW

PINK

PURPLE

WHITE

BLACK

GREEN

BLUE

ORANGE

Ellie Changes Colour

Cover design by Dawn Riley
Written and illustrated by Dawn Riley

First published 2017 by
Riley Hooper Ltd

Printed in the United States of America

ISBN-13   978-0473386788
ISBN-10   047338678X

www.ingramcontent.com/pod-product-compliance
Lightning Source LLC
Chambersburg PA
CBHW040347060426
42445CB00029B/36